MW01242789

More Praise for
Leading The Agile Enterprise

Dr. Ferreira's handbook, *Leading the Agile Enterprise*, maps a clear pathway from the history of agile to the future of business. If you're interested in understanding how innovation, leadership, and agility intersect, then grab a copy to read.

–Evan Leybourn, Founder, Business Agility Institute

Agile has become a global movement that is transforming all aspects of our work. In this book, Gail starts with the history and goes into ultramodern views of scaling agile in complex organizations. If your team or organization is looking at adopting simple but powerful scaling principles for value, this is the right book. Gail clearly answers how to provide instant, frictionless, clear value at scale.

–Kamal Manglani, Enterprise Agile Transformation Leader

Dr. Gail Ferreira's *Leading the Agile Enterprise: The Essential Guide to Lean Agile Teams, Value Streams, Programs, and Portfolios* is a must read for making sense of enterprise agile leadership. The book provides a thorough background and in-depth analysis of agile, leadership, innovation drivers, and more. It discusses business value and a long-term view of agile. I find the discussion on innovation illuminating: The CEO goes home and wonders how the heck people like Steve Jobs ever made money by innovating. Innovation happens every day, in every organization. It's just that too often it goes unnoticed. I highly recommend reading this guide to get an understanding of the agile history, progress, and future.

–Michael Nir, Keynote Speaker, Best-Selling Author, and Lean Agile Inspiration Expert

It's not easy to find a comprehensive, end-to-end guide on both historical and modern agile concepts that easily summarizes what twenty-first-century leadership needs to understand to guide their organizations into a fast-paced future. Dr. Gail Ferreira's *Leading the Agile Enterprise: The Essential Guide to Lean Agile Teams, Value Streams, Programs, and Portfolios* provides today's leadership with the perfect jumping-off point for understanding the evolution of organizational adaptation techniques and where they should focus to lead tomorrow's competitive landscape.

–Robert M. Woods, National Agile Practice Director, Leading Industry Speaker, Author, and Mentor

LEADING
THE
AGILE
ENTERPRISE

The Essential Guide to Lean Agile Teams,
Value Streams, Programs, and Portfolios

Leading The Agile Enterprise - The Essential Guide to Lean Agile Teams, Value Streams, Programs, and Portfolios
Copyright © 2018 Gail Ferreira

Prima Leader, Inc.

No part of this book may be reproduced in any form or by any electronic or mechanical means including information storage and retrieval systems, without permission in writing from the author. The only exception is by a reviewer, who may quote short excerpts in a published review.

The information presented herein represents the views of the author as of the date of publication. This book is presented for informational purposes only. Due to the rate at which conditions change, the author reserves the right to alter and update her opinions at any time. While every attempt has been made to verify the information in this book, the author does not assume any responsibility for errors, inaccuracies, or omissions.

Book design by:
Arbor Services, Inc.
www.arborservices.co/

Printed in the United States of America

Leading The Agile Enterprise - The Essential Guide to Lean Agile Teams, Value Streams, Programs, and Portfolios
Gail Ferreira

1. Title 2. Author 3. Self-Help

Library of Congress Control Number: 2018939933
ISBN 13: 978-0-692-10084-4

LEADING THE
AGILE
ENTERPRISE

*The Essential Guide to Lean Agile Teams,
Value Streams, Programs, and Portfolios*

GAIL FERREIRA

Prima Leader, Inc.

Contents

Foward

Change has always been a constant in business. The difference in the Internet age with disruption becoming the norm not the exception, organization agility has become a core competency for the modern enterprise. To meet the challenge of change, leaders must learn continuously and be ready to adapt their approach to guide their organizations through constant change. Embracing agile and lean represents one of the most common changes established organizations must navigate, and how leaders lead will determine whether such a transition will succeed or fail.

In *Leading the Agile Enterprise*, Dr. Gail Ferreira provides a solid foundation across a broad set critical knowledge area that leaders must navigate in order to foster organizational agility. This book provides a condensed primer explaining why organizations are driven to change, and the variety of approaches leaders can use to navigate the turbulence a change such as agile transformation creates. Readers are also oriented to the economic and social factors that are challenging the status quo, answering the critical question, "Why do we need to change?"

There are many books to choose from that go deeper into the spectrum of topics Dr. Ferreira touches in *Leading the Agile Enterprise*. For the time-constrained leader looking for a resource that will orient them to the task of change in a short, to-the-point format, this book is a great choice.

Dr. Stephen Mayner
SAFe Fellow
Scaled Agile, Inc.

Introduction

The world of business is changing at a rate humans have never before witnessed.

New technologies, new approaches, and new challenges confront leaders before the previous wave of change has been dealt with. But at the same time, consumer products, especially computer software programs that typically involve millions of lines of code, are becoming increasingly complex.

To balance the acceleration of business with its increasing complexity, the agile methodology emerged. It has worked brilliantly with small teams of five or ten people writing a software program for a customer. In fact, it's worked so well that the agile approach has expanded to larger teams, entire organizations, and businesses well beyond the software industry.

In a small team of only a few people, the agile approach is essentially leaderless. The team members work together democratically because that's what small teams can do.

3

But when an organization of many hundreds or thousands of employees adopts the agile approach, you need leaders who can initiate, direct, and manage this new and sometimes unfamiliar culture.

This book is intended to serve as a guide for the leader of the agile enterprise.

It's not a theoretical treatise but a practical, hands-on resource that will help any leader of any agile company, division, or project team understand the agile approach and leverage it to create the most value possible. It reveals the key elements of the agile methodology as they relate to scaling up to larger enterprises, and can help you, the leader, guide your organization to robust growth and higher profits.

Ready? Let's get started!

Chapter 1:

The Emergence of Agile

It's no secret that today's business environment is more competitive and faster moving than ever before. Markets are bigger and more complex. The rate of change of technology is accelerating. The product or process that was cutting edge last year may be obsolete tomorrow. Customers expect more, and if you don't deliver, they'll broadcast their unhappiness on social media for the world to see. Your employees are more diverse than ever and want to accomplish more than punching a clock and taking home a paycheck.

For your company, these developments could be good news—but only if you're committed to riding the waves of change rather than allowing yourself to be swamped by them.

If you're agile—a powerful concept that's landed in the consciousness of corporate leaders only recently—you can leverage change to your advantage.

If you're rigid, or oblivious to current business conditions, you'll find yourself under water.

The performance of your organization starts with your business systems, and how they are constructed and managed.

Systems Management

In its strictest interpretation, *systems management* refers to enterprise-wide administration of distributed systems with a special focus on computer network management. It has encompassed a variety of different tasks required to monitor and manage information technology (IT) systems and resolve IT problems. These include but aren't limited to the management of hardware asset inventory and configuration; networks, servers, storage, and printers; application software; network security; backup systems; and processes to generate and track trouble tickets and resolve problems.

In its broader sense, systems management refers to how you treat an organization as a set of distinct parts that together form a complex whole. Some of the parts include an organization's assets, employees, information, products, and resources, which together form a complex whole. It stipulates an organization engages in three primary activities: input, process (or throughput), and output. While the components of these three parts depend on the nature of your business, generally "input" includes capital, raw materials, and technology. "Process" may mean either manufacturing or, in service industries, those activities related to human training and management. "Output" consists of the products or services that can be offered for sale.

If the system isn't highly efficient and doesn't produce enough value to earn a profit, then the organization will wither and die. In an open system, success depends on the use of feedback response, from both internal and external sources, to aid in correcting or minimizing errors when executing business operations.

To give a simple example, if your bakery produces cakes, and your customers tell you the cakes tend to be too dry, then you need to adjust your business system to produce moister cakes. This may involve buying a different type of flour (input), baking the cakes differently (process), or shipping them more quickly to the customers (output).

The useful thing about systems is that once you've got them working properly, you can scale them up. If you can successfully bake one hundred cakes that are identical and of uniform quality, then you can scale up and produce one thousand cakes or one hundred thousand cakes that are exactly the same as the first one hundred. The trick is to make sure your cost per cake goes *down* as you scale *up*. In the pages ahead, we'll discuss scaling in more depth.

Systems Development Life Cycle (SDLC)

Also referred to as the application development life cycle, this concept, which has its origins in software development, is narrowly defined as a process used in the development, creation, and maintenance of an information system.

1. The SDLC has five phases:
2. Planning
3. Analysis
4. Design
5. Implementation
6. Maintenance

It's easy to see that these five phases could apply to any enterprise that creates and sells a product or service. For example, let's say your company is launching a national division that provides plumbers for residential repairs. The idea is that the customer can go online and book a plumber. To accomplish this goal, you need to set up a nationwide online booking system. You:

1. Plan how the booking system will benefit your new division and how it will work.

2. Analyze the cost and expected performance.

3. Design the system, both as it appears on the customer's screen and the back-office operations that link it to individual plumbers and the sales operation.

4. Implement the system, first with beta testing and then with actual customers.

5. Maintain the system, which includes making improvements and working out any glitches.

With an agile approach—which we'll dive into soon—step #5 is the most important, because the first iteration you launch may be a "minimal viable product" (MVP) that you intend to refine over time as the system gains real-world experience.

Project Management Body of Knowledge (PMBOK)

In project management, a project is a temporary endeavor undertaken to create a unique product, service, or result. For any project to be properly developed and managed, it's a good idea to have a road map showing you how others have done it. The Project Management Body of Knowledge is a set of common guidelines and terminology for project management. This body of knowledge, which evolves over time, is presented in a book entitled *A Guide to the Project Management Body of Knowledge* (also called simply the *PMBOK Guide*). The sixth edition was released in 2017. The *PMBOK Guide* has resulted from work overseen by the Project Management Institute (PMI), which offers the CAPM and PMP certifications.

The book describes both the project management life cycle and the project life cycle, and for the first time it includes an "Agile Practice Guide."

It describes the five "process groups," which are similar to the five phases of the systems development life cycle (SDLC), as described earlier in this book. They are:

1. Initiating
2. Planning
3. Executing
4. Monitoring and Controlling
5. Closing

There are also ten "knowledge areas." They refer to the project management of the following functional areas:

1. Integration—the individual tasks holding the overall project together
2. Scope—the work included within the project
3. Schedule or time—the start and finish dates for each task

4. Cost—the budget for each task
5. Quality—established during project planning and specified within the project management plan
6. Human resources—getting the appropriate people involved
7. Communications—keeping all stakeholders well informed throughout the project
8. Risk—identifying, planning, and controlling for things that could go wrong
9. Procurement—hiring any outside contractors
10. Stakeholders—actively managing their expectations during the project life cycle

Projects come in all shapes and sizes. The development of a software application for a business process, the design and construction of a skyscraper, the launch of a new product, the deployment of troops overseas to complete a mission—all are projects that must be expertly managed to deliver on-time, on-budget results. If a project achieves its stated objectives within its schedule and budget, then it's a success.

Lean

Derived from the Toyota Production System (TPS), which beginning in 1948 and was pioneered by Taiichi Ohno, Eiji Toyoda, and other Japanese industrial engineers, the concept of "lean" manufacturing was given its name by John Krafcik in his 1988 article, "Triumph of the Lean Production System."

You can look at lean in two ways.

The first way is that lean focuses on the *elimination of waste* from the production process. Waste, or *muda* in Japanese, is defined as anything that doesn't add value to the product *in the judgment of the customer.* As waste is eliminated, value is added.

Waste can take many forms, which in the Toyota system are grouped into three classes.

Muri focuses on the preparation and planning of the process, or what work can be avoided proactively by design.

Mura focuses on the elimination of fluctuation at the scheduling or operations level, such as quality and volume.

Muda is revealed after the process is operating and is dealt with reactively. It is detected through variation in output.

In practice, *muda* gets the most attention because it focuses on a system that's operating, and the efforts to make it more efficient. Originally, Toyota identified seven types of *muda:*

1. Transport (the wasted energy of moving material before or after processing)
2. Inventory (all raw materials, the work in process, and unsold finished products)
3. Motion (people or equipment moving before or after processing)
4. Waiting (any nonproductive time for any reason)
5. Overproduction (making too much relative to demand)
6. Overprocessing (wasted iterations or steps in the process)
7. Defects (products that cannot be sold by reason of unsuitability)

Since then, others have added additional sources of waste, such as the waste of making a product that does not precisely meet the customer's expectations, the waste of underutilizing a talented worker, or the waste of insufficiently training a worker.

The second way to look at lean is through the lens of the Toyota Production System and what has become known as *kaizen*, which is the Japanese word for "improvement" but which has come to mean more specifically the process of *continuous incremental improvement*. In business, *kaizen* refers to any and all activities that continuously improve the performance of the business and involve all employees from the CEO to the assembly line workers. It can apply to any process, from the supply chain to marketing to finance. The methodology focuses on observing problems or waste, making changes, monitoring the results, and then repeating the process. The drawing up of expansive plans and comprehensive advance project scheduling can be replaced by many smaller mini-projects, which can be rapidly adjusted as new improvements are suggested.

One of the industrial hallmarks of lean manufacturing is the concept of *just in time*, whereby instead of procuring and warehousing raw materials and parts well in advance—a form of wasted capital and labor—the parts required for a project ideally arrive at the moment they're needed for processing. This ideal scenario has gotten a boost from the growth of the Internet of Things, which allows the precise real-time tracking of any object over great distances. If an assembly manager needs to know the location of the windshields for the up-coming shift's quota of pickup trucks, he or she need only consult the company intranet to learn the exact arrival time. Good *flow* describes a system where work moves steadily and predictably, allowing it to complete *just in time*, whereas bad *flow* describes a system where work stops and starts frequently.

The Emergence of Agile

From these concepts the idea of agile emerged. Its origins have been well documented: In February 2001, at The Lodge at Snowbird ski resort in the Wasatch Mountains of Utah, seventeen software engineers brainstormed and wrote what they called the "Agile Manifesto":

We are uncovering better ways of developing software by doing it and helping others do it. Through this work we have come to value:

Individuals and interactions over processes and tools.
Working software over comprehensive documentation.
Customer collaboration over contract negotiation.
Responding to change over following a plan.
That is, while there is value in the items on the right, we value the items on the left more.

© 2001, the Agile Manifesto authors

It's very simple, but it's helped create a new approach to process formulation, to project management, and even to the business management of large-scale enterprises.

The problem they were trying to solve was that software is unlike most other manufactured products. A complete software application consists of millions of lines of code, and ideally you'll want every line to work perfectly. Luckily, most software applications can be built as a *minimal viable product* that's the bare-bones version of the intended product but which functions sufficiently for the customer to test it. So you build the application in *iterations*, a little at a time. You test each iteration before adding more to it. It would be like if you could build a house one room at a time, and while the customer lived in the completed rooms you kept adding more rooms until the customer had an entire house.

Remember that many old-school manufactured products cannot be delivered in iterations. For example, consider the Boeing 787 Dreamliner. Each plane is made from 2.3 million individual parts. The prototype aircraft was first flown on December 15, 2009, for three hours. On September 25, 2011, Boeing delivered the first passenger-ready 787 to All Nippon Airways. While of course the plane had undergone extensive flight testing, the customer *did not take possession until the product was perfect*. There could be no "minimal viable product." On delivery, the plane either worked perfectly or it didn't.

But for any situation in which customer feedback can be a part of the process, and a product or service can be developed in workable iterations with continuous improvements, then the agile approach has real value.

Two Types of Organizations: Learning and Chaordic

The agile enterprise shares much in common with two types of organizations, *learning* and *chaordic*.

Leaders of agile enterprises have moved beyond familiar best practices in order to build *learning organizations* that can adapt quickly to changing conditions. This has become a critical business strategy, helping companies both stay competitive and improve employee engagement.

Bersin Research, an independent HR-focused analyst group at Deloitte, has constructed a maturity model that supports organizations seeking to evolve to the next level of organizational learning. According to Bersin's High-Impact Learning Organization Maturity Model, as learning organizations, businesses place in one of four distinct levels:

Level 1: Episodic/Programmatic—learning is incidental or in response to an emerging need.

Level 2: Responsive/Contextualized—formalized training is led by a centralized learning and development (L&D) team.

Level 3: Continuous/Empowering—talent development is a core competency of management throughout the company, and key performance indicators are measured.

Level 4: Anticipatory/Flow—here, both executives and employees are aligned around continuous learning, bolstered by an agile corporate structure and the use of strategic tools for learning and development.

The term chaordic organization has a specific origin. Formulated by Dee Hock and others in forming the VISA organization in 1970, the term "chaord" is formed from the words "chaos" and "order." In "The Chaordic Organization: Out of Control and Into Order," Hock wrote, "At the same time, the core of the [chaordic] enterprise has no knowledge of or authority over a vast number of the constituent parts. No part knows the whole, the whole does not know all the parts and none has any need to. The entirety, like all chaords—including those you call body, brain, and biosphere—is largely self-regulating."

Why a chaordic organization? Because Hock and others realized that the management of a global financial services company on the scale of VISA would be impossible with a traditional Industrial Age hierarchical command structure. As he wrote, the organization needed to be "self–organizing, adaptive, non-linear, and complex"—in other words, while very large, it had to be agile, both in its behavior and its structure.

Chapter 2:

Leadership in the Twenty-first Century

Every organization, even the most democratic, needs a leader—someone who has both the authority and the ability to settle disputes, articulate the organization's mission and vision, make decisions about resource allocation, and defend against attacks.

Being an effective leader is a tricky business. If you're too forceful and listen too much to the voice in your head, you run the risk of being out of touch and having your stakeholders think you're a dictator. If you're too accommodating to others and spend too much time listening, you run the risk of being indecisive and having your stakeholders think you're timid. It's not good to be too analytical, too touchy-feely, or too much of a hundred other character traits.

In the real world, every leader is different. Each leader needs to know what works for his or her individual personality, and what the organization needs from them to achieve sustained success.

This chapter is about leadership and how it's never a one-size-fits-all proposition. A person who is an effective leader at one organization may be ineffective at another. It's all about aligning the personality of the leader with the culture and goals of the organization. When you have alignment, you have a greater chance for success.

The Leadership Culture

Every organization—from the US Army to the funkiest startup in San Francisco—has its own culture, which includes how leaders are chosen and how they do their jobs. Some are hierarchical, while others are democratic. Some are agile and responsive to change, while others hew closely to what's tried and true. Some organizations are controlled by a single founding family, and others are guided by investors.

In any organization, the leadership culture is the totality of its human behaviors, beliefs, and practices, shaped by the formal organizational structure or even the organization's bylaws. It's the way people interact, get information, influence others, and make decisions. In the early stages of an organization's life, decisions and behaviors are driven by the conscious and unconscious beliefs of the leader. When these behaviors are repeated over time, they become leadership practices. When more time passes, these entrenched practices become the leadership culture.

While every leadership culture is unique, we can classify them according to some general distinctions of type. The nonprofit Center for Creative Leadership places leadership cultures in three basic categories:

- **Dependent leadership** cultures operate with the belief that people in authority are responsible for leadership. This is the traditional hierarchical system, where the leader is the legally empowered authority standing on top of the pyramid.

- **Independent leadership** cultures operate with the belief that leadership emerges out of individual expertise and heroic action. This is like a governing body, such as a legislature, where policy is debated among individuals with their own agendas to eventually reach mutual agreement.

- **Interdependent leadership** cultures operate with the belief that leadership is a collective activity to the benefit of the organization as a whole. The CCL calls this "boundary spanning," or the capability of individuals to create direction, alignment, and commitment across boundaries in service of a higher vision or goal. Here, the individual's self-interest, while not abandoned, takes second place to the interests of the group.

In an agile organization, you're going to want to have a leadership culture of interdependence, in which every individual acts both with self-interest and with community interest.

Servant Leadership

The concept of the servant leader is an ancient one.

Consider this passage from the *Tao Te Ching*, attributed to Lao-Tzu, who is believed to have lived in China between 570 BCE and 490 BCE:

The highest type of ruler is one of whose existence the people are barely aware.

Next comes one whom they love and praise.

Next comes one whom they fear.

Next comes one whom they despise and defy.

In the modern era, the term is credited to Robert K. Greenleaf in his essay "The Servant as Leader," which he first published in 1970. In that essay, Greenleaf said:

"The servant-leader is servant first . . . It begins with the natural feeling that one wants to serve, to serve first. Then conscious choice brings one to aspire to lead. That person is sharply different from one who is leader first, perhaps because of the need to assuage an unusual power drive or to acquire material possessions."

Servant leadership can perhaps be put into the context of the leader as someone whose primary task is to *help subordinates perform their tasks*. Obviously, this doesn't mean that the CEO should perform the actual work of an employee (although if you've ever watched the TV show *Undercover Boss*, sometimes getting down into the trenches is a positive experience for a CEO!). It means that the CEO is responsible for ensuring employees:

- ✓ Know and understand the mission and vision of the organization
- ✓ Have the tools and equipment necessary to do their jobs
- ✓ Have the proper training to do their jobs
- ✓ Are engaged with the organization and are willing to give their best effort
- ✓ Are free from harassment or other inappropriate or illegal acts by others

✓ Are fairly compensated in a manner that's competitive with the marketplace

There are more, but from this short list it's easy to see that any leader who makes these goals his or her priority will have little free time to engage in self-aggrandizement!

Ubuntu

Ubuntu is an Nguni Bantu term meaning "humanity." It's part of the Zulu phrase *umuntu ngumuntu ngabantu*, which literally means that a person is a person through other people. Ubuntu has its roots in humanist African philosophy, where the idea of community is one of the building blocks of society.

By saying that "my humanity exists in your humanity" or "my excellence is found in your excellence," in the agile enterprise the Ubuntu philosophy recognizes we're all in this together, emphasizes the value of human dignity, and directly relates to organizations that are seeking synergy between all their parts and people in their organization. Focusing on collaboration in economic, social, and environmental situations helps move away from the "us vs. them" mentality so prevalent in corporations, politics, and traditionally led organizations.

Ubuntu teaches us to be open minded and free from preconceptions. Leaders need to discard their inherent prejudices (we all have them!) and look at their leadership approach through a broader, more objective lens. It advocates for the leader to be in the present moment rather than trapped by past processes, experiences, and inherent biases.

A fully aware leader is able to enhance individual and team performance by being open to feedback from others and engaging in meaningful relationships with followers. In doing so, they help create an environment where employees feel safe to express their opinions and openly discuss all issues.

Make no mistake: This is not just a feel-good philosophy. For the agile enterprise seeking to compete at the highest levels in an increasingly disrupted marketplace, Ubuntu has a lot to offer that can lead to better organizational performance and higher profits.

Compassionate Leadership

The dictionary defines "compassion" as "a feeling of deep sympathy and sorrow for another who is stricken by misfortune, accompanied by a strong desire to alleviate the suffering." As a leadership approach, this would seem to be a far cry from the sneering viewpoint offered by Gordon Gekko in the 1987 film *Wall Street*: "Greed is good." In fact, multiple studies have shown how crucial compassion is to effective, agile leadership.

Christina Boedker of the Australian School of Business conducted a research study on the link between leadership and organizational performance. From data collected from more than 5,600 people in seventy-seven organizations, she concluded that of the wide range of skills needed by an effective leader, the ability to be empathetic and compassionate, "to understand people's motivators, hopes and difficulties and to create the right support mechanism to allow people to be as good as they can be," had the greatest correlation with profitability and productivity.

Likewise, a study by Google on what constitutes a great leader revealed that employees appreciate managers who show concern for them both personally and professionally. In contrast, the leader's technical expertise was surprisingly irrelevant. As Laszlo Bock, former senior vice president of people operations at Google, told *The New York Times*, "It turns out that that's absolutely the least important thing. It's important, but pales in comparison. Much more important is just making that connection and being accessible."

The number one most desirable habit of a Google manager? "Be a good coach."

Compassionate leaders consistently boost employee morale, employee productivity, and bottom-line profitability. This is even more true for frontline managers who, more than the CEO, interact with employees on a day-to-day basis.

Emergent Leadership

In this leadership approach, rather than a group member being appointed or elected to the leadership role, leadership develops over time as a result of the group's day-to-day interaction.

This approach has been tried in several big companies, most notably the online shoe retailer Zappos. In 2015, after a few years of experimentation, Zappos launched its high-profile adoption of *holacracy*. This organizational model proposed by software engineer Brian J.

Robertson distributes decision-making authority in self-organizing circles made up of employees without formal job descriptions, with each circle arranged around a purpose statement. These experimental approaches, according to Zappos CEO Tony Hsieh, enable every employee to act as a "human sensor," and the organization as a whole to be more adaptable, innovative, and resilient.

In May 2017, Hsieh told an interviewer from McKinsey & Co., "Imagine a greenhouse with lots of plants, and each plant represents an employee. Maybe at a typical company, the CEO is the tallest, strongest plant that the other plants aspire to one day become. That's not how I think of my role. Instead, I think of my role as the architect of the greenhouse, and to help figure out the right conditions within the greenhouse to enable all of the other plants to flourish and thrive."

Hsieh described the Zappos company culture as being like 1,500 entrepreneurs united under a common set of values. This, he says, is the best way to cultivate and harness the "collective intelligence" of the group.

Transformational Leadership

In 1978, presidential biographer and leadership expert James Mac-Gregor Burns defined the concept of a "transformational leader" as exhibiting traits and behaviors to inspire and motivate a team or organization to rally around a common vision or goal. He defined transformational leadership as a process where "leaders and their followers raise one another to higher levels of morality and motivation." These behaviors and traits include intellectual stimulation, inspirational motivation, charisma, and individual consideration for each team or group member.

Transformational leaders seek to:

✓ Identify what needs to change.

✓ Solve problems by seeking new solutions.

✓ Work to change the existing system.

✓ Maximize their teams' capacity and capability.

They challenge traditional assumptions and don't accept answers like, "Because this is the way we've always done it."

Transformational leadership is often contrasted with *transactional leadership*, which focuses on the roles of organization, supervision, and group performance. Transactional leaders are concerned about the status quo and day-to-day progress toward goals. Compliance by followers is promoted through both rewards and punishments. Instead of looking to change the future, transactional leaders seek to keep things the same. They pay close attention to the work of subordinates in order to find faults and deviations.

Can one person be both? In fact, Steve Jobs has been described as being both transformative and transactional. He was a visionary who was obsessed with the details of Apple's products. He inspired his employees and also browbeat them. He worked to change existing systems while sending Apple's manufacturing to China. "Companies once felt an obligation to support American workers, even when it wasn't the best financial choice," said Betsey Stevenson, a former chief economist at the Labor Department, to *The New York Times*.

"That's disappeared. Profits and efficiency have trumped generosity." In fact, when President Obama asked Steve Jobs if any of those manufacturing jobs were ever coming back to the United States, the reply was, "Those jobs aren't coming back."

Change Management Leadership

Change management is a structured approach to transitioning individuals, teams, and organizations from an existing unacceptable state to a desired future state, with the purpose of fulfilling or implementing a strategy and vision. From the perspective of assuring robust investor returns, it's the continuous process of aligning an organization with its marketplace in a way that is more responsive and effective than both the previous version of the organization and its current competitors.

The process of change can be fraught with tension because there may be internal winners and losers. Losers fear their capacity for control and influence will diminish. To protect their existing power, instead of bringing fresh ideas to the table, those who feel threatened may seek to undermine the leader and his or her agenda.

Numerous frameworks have been proposed for managing disruptive change. For example, Jeff Hiatt, a former engineer and program manager for Bell Labs, proposed the ADKAR model as a way to address employee resistance to organizational change. In this model, he identified five building blocks that bring about successful change:

Awareness – Team members must be made aware of the necessity for change.

Desire – Team members must have the desire to support and participate in the change.

Knowledge – Team members must have the knowledge of how to change.

Ability – Team members must have the ability to acquire new skills and implement the change at the required performance level.

Reinforcement – Leaders must ensure reinforcement of the change over time.

Leaders who succeed at change management do so by being skilled diplomats and by knowing how to apply pressure as needed. Getting the trust and alignment needed to implement change can be a difficult task, and a leader needs to develop a rapport with key people within each power center by learning what is important to them as individuals and as a group within their respective cultures.

Leaders who successfully transform their organizations are respected and sought after. Rather than being destroyed by disruption within their industries, their organizations find ways to leverage those changes.

Chapter 3:

Drive to Innovate

Innovation.

For many leaders, this is a scary word. It conjures up images of high-tech Silicon Valley nerds hunched over glowing computer screens or laboratory benches, working feverishly to invent something astonishing that the world has never seen before. Meanwhile, the hapless CEO watches as the project investment money flows down the drain like water. As the days, weeks, and months tick by with no market-shattering breakthrough, the CEO is torn between throwing more money at the problem or cutting the company's losses and categorizing the whole crazy idea as a colossal waste of money. The CEO goes home and wonders how the heck people like Steve Jobs ever made money by innovating.

In reality, innovation happens every day, in every organization. It's just that too often it goes unnoticed.

The invention of new shiny objects represents only one small corner of the vast innovation universe. And while such projects may capture headlines and the public's imagination, 99% of all innovation happens quietly, out of sight of the public, in areas of organizations that you'd never suspect could be centers of new ideas.

Here are a few examples of innovation at XYZ Company:

- In the human resources department, a manager creates a program whereby employees can work from home two days a week. This is a significant innovation that will boost employee engagement, reduce attrition by employees with young children, and attract employees with higher qualifications, which adds value to the company.

- In the shipping department, an employee suggests attaching a GPS tracking device to every outgoing pallet of goods. This innovation allows the order fulfillment manager to precisely predict when the shipment will arrive at its destination and alert them to any delays in real time.

- On the assembly line, a worker finds a way to perform routine maintenance on a machine in one minute's less time than was previously possible. This savings of one minute per shift boosts productivity and speeds up production time. The cost savings translate to higher profits.

- In the marketing department, an employee takes real-time customer feedback from social media and forwards it to the product design team, who make tweaks to the product before each new iteration goes into production. This agility means the company can more closely meet its customers' expectations while still maintaining a steady flow of product to market.

These are all innovations that either save the company money or directly boost revenues (either outcome is equally favorable). They are not glitzy or glamorous, and aren't the result of a structured "innovation initiative" promulgated by the executive suite. They happen every day, without fanfare, in companies large and small.

Yes, it's true that some innovation is the result of deliberately constructed innovation programs. For example, in the pharmaceutical industry, new inventions are the source of all future profits. But make no mistake: These are big, expensive programs. A recent study by the Tufts Center for the Study of Drug Development (CSDD) puts the cost of developing a prescription drug that gains market approval at $2.6 billion. This total is based on an average investment cost of $1.4 billion, to which you have to add an estimated $1.2 billion in lost returns that investors don't get on their money during the decade a new drug typically spends in development. The study then adds $312 million spent on post-approval development—studies to test dosage strengths, formulations, and new indications—for a life cycle cost of $2.9 billion.

These are big numbers at companies that have long traditions of new product development. But drug companies aren't at the top of the list of investors in innovation. Guess what company currently spends the most on research & development?

Pfizer? Tesla Motors? Apple?

The answer may surprise you: it's Amazon.com, which according to Bloomberg spent $17.4 billion on R&D over the twelve months ending in March 2017. There's one caveat: Amazon doesn't categorize

R&D spending as a separate line item. Instead, it has a section under operating expenses for "technology and content," which its financial reports describe thusly:

"Technology costs consist principally of research and development activities including payroll and related expenses for employees involved in application, production, maintenance, operation, and development of new and existing products and services, as well as AWS [Amazon Web Services] and other technology infrastructure costs. Content costs consist principally of payroll and related expenses for employees involved in category expansion, editorial content, buying, and merchandising selection."

In other words, Amazon doesn't look at innovation as being solely the process of inventing cool new stuff. At Amazon, innovation is pursued everywhere throughout the company to serve a variety of functions, most of which its customers are not consciously aware.

The Four Levels of Innovation

Not all innovation is created equal. Generally, you can place or rank an innovation along a four-point scale.

1. **Valueless.** Just because something is *new* or *different* doesn't make it *valuable*. You can "innovate" by putting fins on a car, but unless you're adding value that a customer will pay for, the fins will cost you money while adding nothing to your sales. Beware of pointless innovations that customers don't value or don't reduce your supply chain costs.

2. **Incremental.** This is an innovation that takes a small step forward. It may or may not be known to the customer. It could be a cost-cutting idea on the assembly line, or a better way to process insurance claims, or a better battery in your smartphone. Over time, incremental innovations can really add up—they are what made Toyota the world's biggest carmaker during most of the past few decades.

3. **Breakthrough.** These are the big splashy innovations that can change the marketplace. The Tesla electric car has reshaped the automobile industry. The Apple iPod revolutionized music storing and listening. Before that, it was the CD, and before the CD came cassette tapes and vinyl LPs. Breakthroughs can happen in human resources, such as the 2010 decision to allow gays to serve openly in the military; in the supply chain, such as the growth of the Internet of Things (IoT), which allows the tracking of individual parts along the chain; or in marketing, with the emergence of social media and "permission" marketing.

4. **Disruptive.** Some innovations are so powerful they don't only change markets, they demolish them. Uber decimated the taxi industry. Amazon crushed the bookstore industry and has put a big dent in traditional department stores. The wireless phone has eliminated public pay phones, reduced home landlines, and even changed how we pay for things we buy. Netflix wiped out the bricks-and-mortar DVD rental industry and its biggest player, Blockbuster.

Many disruptive innovations, such as Netflix, are initially dismissed by competitors who are too entrenched and have invested too much in their business infrastructure. These newcomers start small, but like a snowball rolling downhill, can soon become an avalanche. Competitors that are agile can adapt and continue to compete. Those that aren't agile can get buried.

Surprisingly, agility is not always related to size. Consider General Motors which, when it went bankrupt in 2009, was the textbook example of a paralyzed, arthritic, sclerotic dinosaur. Miraculously it reinvented itself and became profitable in 2010. Today it ranks number three in sales. Its products are well regarded, and some are even innovative.

Planned Innovation and Spontaneous Innovation

When a company is taking stock of its approach toward innovation, it first needs to understand the difference between *planned innovation* and what I call *spontaneous innovation.*

Planned innovation is exactly what it sounds like: a consistent, well-funded program to create new products and processes that will help the organization fulfill its mission. This is what Apple, Volkswagen AG, Amazon, and the other big R&D spenders do. It's innovation specifically designed to solve a known problem. For example, at Tesla Motors, a known problem is the manufacturing cost of electric batteries, and the company is making a dedicated effort to solve this problem.

What's more interesting from a perspective of the agile enterprise is spontaneous innovation.

This is the process of encouraging, identifying, evaluating, and implementing accidental or unforeseen innovations that can happen at any time and at any level in an organization. Examples include those cited earlier in this chapter, where the worker on the shipping dock or in human resources finds a way to complete a task more efficiently or at lower cost, and his or her idea is noticed, taken seriously, evaluated, and implemented by those in a position to make such decisions. This is the type of innovation that can take place in any company in any industry.

Spontaneous innovation is related to the concept of *kaizen*, identified with the Toyota Production System, which I touched upon earlier in the book. Within the TPS, one of the foundations of a culture of continuous improvement, is a well-entrenched program of employee suggestions. To succeed, such a program must be fully integrated into the fabric of worker development and support. It starts with a culture committed to building collaboration, teamwork, and worker empowerment.

The empowerment of employees, and their willingness to offer new ideas, works only in organizations where methods and tasks have been clearly defined. Personal initiative must be encouraged within clearly defined boundaries. People need to be properly trained, equipped, and supported.

While Toyota has had its share of breakthrough innovations such as the Prius, the first successful hybrid vehicle, the company is built on an ethos of *continuous incremental improvement*, which is what the word *kaizen* has come to mean in popular culture. It's rooted in the Toyota Creative Ideas and Suggestions System (TCISS), which encourages employees to suggest improvements at work.

The system was introduced in May 1951 by managing director Eiji Toyoda, who borrowed the idea from a Ford Motor Company plant he had visited a year earlier. A suggestion system employed by Ford placed emphasis on supporting its improvement activities through opinions not only from the management side but from the factory floor. As Eiji Toyoda himself wrote, "As the years passed, the TCISS became steadily more productive. Teams were formed to create ideas for improvements, and the suggestions themselves became more substantial, as all employees were encouraged to review their jobs constantly and implement improvements."

Today, TCISS generates millions of ideas per year. Every year, the company reportedly receives an average of forty-eight new ideas from each employee, of which (according to Chuck Yorke and Norman Bodek's book *All You Gotta Do Is Ask*) nine are eventually adopted. Clearly, the program has strong elements of planned innovation because it's a well-established part of the company's everyday operations, as it should be. Toyota has been doing it for so long that the rate of new ideas has become predictable.

But at the end of the day it's a culture that's designed to capture purely spontaneous innovations because the problems for which solutions are offered aren't identified and funded in the same way as, for example, the quest for a new pharmaceutical. In effect, every Toyota employee acts like a "waste policeman," charged with identifying any process that could be improved or have value added.

Many companies have robust employee suggestion programs, and from them they get ideas that add value, cut expenses, and boost profits. To not have such a program is to leave money on the table.

The Components of Innovation

To reap the rewards of sustained innovation, organizations need to meet three basic qualifications.

1. **Leadership.** The culture of any company is defined at the top. Innovation must be valued, given oversight, recognized, and when necessary, funded. The high value placed on innovation must be communicated across the organization.

2. **Structure.** Innovators—whether they're working in a funded lab or dropping a note into the employee suggestion box—must know that the organization is equipped to receive and process their idea. Too often, innovation exists only as a vague item on a memo. Accenture notes that 72 percent of companies allow innovations to languish because there is no formalized process or organizational home for such initiatives. And according to an exploratory study of more than thirty companies in the United States and Europe, researchers found that companies generally lack a process to guide innovation. They are leaving money on the table!

3. **Recognition.** Every organization needs an innovation pipeline, and it will remain full if the sources of most new ideas   ordinary

employees—feel as though their contributions are valued. Perhaps surprisingly, studies show that employees are often not interested in monetary reward for their ideas. They contribute because they want to help the organization and feel as though they're doing something positive. There's no faster way to kill an innovation effort than to make employees feel as though their ideas, when submitted, vanish into a black hole of bureaucracy.

For a culture of innovation to thrive—and drive profits—make it sincere, consistent, meaningful, and a source of pride.

Chapter 4:

Identify, Manage, and Enhance Value

In this book I've talked a lot about value. It's a nuanced word, and worth discussing.

Should value be measured in money? Or the emotional effect something has on you? Or some intangible benefit it brings to you, either now or in the future?

For example, if you have a fire extinguisher in your kitchen, it may sit there year after year, untouched. At any given moment, it has no value. It's not doing anything other than taking up space. But it makes you *feel* better. It gives you a sense of security. And if one day you actually have a fire in your kitchen, that fire extinguisher might save your house from burning down. What then would be its value? Well, how valuable is your house?

What *consumers* value is of course a huge question for companies that make products or provide services. In fact, there's no bigger question.

For example, in 1977 Ken Olsen, the president, chairman, and founder of Digital Equipment Corp., said, "There is no reason anyone would want a computer in their home." He didn't see the value because he couldn't imagine what anyone would want to *do* with a computer in their home. People like Steve Jobs saw the value, and as it has turned out, people have found all sorts of things to do with personal computers, from starting home businesses to watching funny kitten videos.

The Brussels-based consultant Pascal Van Cauwenberghe wrote, "There's not just one value or one quality: different stakeholders all value lots of [conflicting] things. Moreover, value is not static. For example: whether I deliver a car [or a software project] next week or in six months can have enormous effects on your valuation of that exact same product."

True! Let's say you're building a Boeing 787 Dreamliner. Many of its 2.3 million parts are made by foreign vendors and delivered to the two assembly plants in Everett, Washington, or North Charleston, South Carolina. For example, as CNN reported, German firm Diehl Luftfahrt Elektronik supplies the main cabin lighting, French firm Messier-Dowty makes the aircraft's landing gear system, Italian firm Alenia Aeronautica makes the center fuselage, Swedish firm Saab Aerostructures supplies the access doors, and Japanese company Jamco makes parts for the galleys, lavatories, and flight deck interiors.

If any one of the roughly one hundred parts suppliers for the 787 Dreamliner fails to deliver the exact part needed, in full and on time, then each airplane, which carries a base price of $146 million, could sit on the factory floor or in the hangar, a massive hunk of metal and carbon fiber that creates no value.

In fact, in January 2013, all operational Boeing 787s were grounded for three months. The problem? A fire hazard in a lithium-ion battery supplied by an overseas vendor. For three long months the fleet of operational 787s sat idle, costing airlines an estimated $1 million per day per aircraft. Once the issue was resolved, the National Transportation Safety Board blamed the battery manufacturer for faults in production, as well as Boeing and the Federal Aviation Administration for poor oversight.

One bad part cost the airlines and Boeing millions of dollars.

Value Management

In many companies, different stakeholders have different opinions on what constitutes value.

The marketing director may place the highest value on capturing market share.

The head of operations may value efficiency and lower costs.

The head of product development may value giving more choices to customers, which drives up costs.

The chief financial officer is concerned with reducing financial risk.

The shareholders want the monetary value of their shares to go up.

These competing groups need a referee, who in theory must be the CEO.

Value management (VM) is concerned with improving and sustaining a desirable balance between the wants and needs of stakeholders and the resources needed to satisfy them. Stakeholder value judgments vary, and VM reconciles differing priorities to deliver best value for all stakeholders.

As the Institute of Value Management wrote, "VM is based on principles of defining and adding measurable value, focusing on objectives before solutions, and concentrating on function to enhance innovation. It uniquely combines within an integrated framework a value focused management style; a positive approach to individual and team motivation; an awareness of the organizational environment; and the effective use of proven methods and tools."

Value Measurement

How is business value defined and measured? The answer depends on the industry and the specific strategic goals of the organization. For example, for a Fortune 50 high-technology firm, innovative new products and services may have the highest weighted value. For biotechnology, some of the highest business value can include drug innovation, quality, patient care, and speed to market. For a financial firm, security and compliance portfolio items may have the highest value, and for mobile products, user interface, portability, and ease of use may have the highest business value.

One way of analyzing and evaluating how and where a business produces value is to take the approach proposed by Ralph Whittle and Conrad B. Mryick in their book *Enterprise Business Architecture: The Formal Link between Strategy and Results* (CRC Press 2004). Here, a "value stream is defined as a chronologically linked succession of activities or processes that create a desired result for a customer, who may be either the ultimate customer or an internal 'end user' of the value stream."

The phrase "concept to cash" is often used to describe everything a value stream must have.

A singular event triggers the flow of value. This event could be the decision to build a product in hopes of finding a buyer, the receipt of a customer purchase order, or the necessity to rebuild a defective product. It ends when some value—a shipment, customer purchase, or solution deployment—has been delivered.

The value stream has a clear objective: to "satisfy or to delight the customer," who in turn will buy the product or service, thereby adding to the organization's revenues. The value streams therefore must be customer centric and dedicated to the efficient and effective delivery of outcomes, results, products, or services.

The *enterprise business architecture* (EBA) is the sum total and arrangement of the enterprise value streams, taking into account their relationships to events that trigger instantiation, internal and external entities, and other enterprise value streams. It's what the enterprise must produce to do all of the things it must to thrive in a competitive environment: deal with its suppliers, compete in a market, satisfy its customers, deal with regulatory agencies, and care for its employees. It is composed of architectures, workflows, and events.

Having fully integrated the EBA to the organization's overall strategy, its integration must be continued with any major initiative that is developed in service of the strategy. A new strategic initiative may require additional architecture elements such as software development, package software configuration, IT architecture build-out, process improvement, organizational architecture development, and security architecture analysis. The EBA model allows the businessperson to define business rules and requirements in one template and in terms that businesspeople can readily understand and leverage.

The tremendous explosion of digital communications in the twenty-first century has shaped enterprise business architecture; in fact, this century has been dubbed the Information Age. It's characterized by the fact that customers can be communicated with by virtually anyone, anytime, and anywhere. In the current era of social media and mobile computing, this means that both a company *and* its competitors can also reach those same customers, anytime and anywhere.

Functional and Process-Based Organizations

This leads us to a discussion of companies being organized on a *functional* vs. *process* basis, and how the balance is shifting toward process.

A functional business orientation organizes a company by making separate departments for all the various functions that share a common purpose, such as production, sales, and maintenance. For example, a company that makes a variety of household products would funnel all the products through specialized procurement, manufacturing, design, sales, and marketing functions. In such a structure, individual workers tend to not be particularly concerned with the other tasks happening in the other departments of the company. Employees working in functional teams have expertise only in their domains, making them less able to tolerate company-wide shifts of direction or culture. The vertical structure of a function-based organization tends toward less transparency, giving rise to rivalries and internal politics. And coordinating development of highly specialized functional units is more challenging.

However, the vertical hierarchy can make decision making comparatively faster. A functional structure can work well when the organization is small in size, communication is fast, management is highly engaged, and the work environment is stable and predictable.

In contrast, a process business orientation means that the company exhibits a cross functional structure where teams consist of members of different functions. For example, a household products company would organize cross-functional teams where each has responsibility for their product line such as floor cleaners, dish soaps, air fresheners, and laundry detergent. Each team is self-contained, having their own designers, marketers, and product development people. By working in cross-functional teams, employees are able to understand the working of other functions. Innovation is valued.

This idea is not new; decades ago the auto giant General Motors organized itself into semiautonomous divisions—Buick, Cadillac, Chevrolet, GMC, Oldsmobile, Pontiac, Hummer, Saturn, and others. However, within these divisions—each of which was big enough to be a major corporation in its own right—plenty of functional siloes made innovation and agility extremely difficult.

In each case, an organization will endeavor to optimize their activities, either within the functional units or for each process. Analysts have suggested that optimizing one functional unit may damage another function (as in a zero-sum relationship), while optimizing business processes across organizational lines lifts the entire company. It has also been suggested that in the Information Age, a functionally centric business model is obsolete, representing an approach characteristic of the Industrial Age. Enterprises in the twenty-first century should evolve toward a process-centric model that is based on value streams. Rather than focusing on tasks, process-focused organizations design and manage end-to-end processes, think in terms of the customer and related goals rather than functional goals, and measure process results rather than department efficiencies. Here, connectedness takes precedence over size, flow over stability, and temporality over spatiality.

Value Stream Mapping

As we've seen, a value stream is a sequence of activities required to design, produce, and provide a specific good or service destined for the customer, and along which information and materials flows. The value stream is a fundamental organizational construct in the scaled agile framework, establishing the focus that allows a lean-agile enterprise to identify and measure the flow of value from sourcing and design to delivery. As an enterprise better understands its value streams, it can marshal resources and attention around them, optimizing them by reducing delays, unnecessary steps, and waste. By doing so, it can continuously reduce and ultimately achieve the lead time for value delivery.

Value streams can be complicated, especially when you try to calculate all the costs that go into creating a product from inception to delivery. After all, creating a product involves nothing but cost until it's delivered to a paying customer. The goal is to keep *adding* value at every step of the value stream. As we know from the Toyota Production System, things that *remove* or *deplete* value include time delays, underutilized talent, wasted materials, added features the customer doesn't value, and poor quality resulting in rejected or returned product.

Value stream mapping is a lean management method for evaluating the existing condition and designing a future condition for the chain of events, in its totality, that take a product or service from its inception all the way to the customer. It's not an entirely new concept; examples of charts showing the flow of information and materials can be seen in a 1918 book by Charles E. Knoeppel called *Installing Efficiency Methods*. At Toyota, it's known as "material-and information-flow mapping." While typically associated with manufacturing, value stream mapping can be used in nearly any system where value is added, such as administrative and office processes, product development, software development, healthcare, service-related industries, supply chain, and logistics.

Value stream maps—which used to be called flow charts—may take the form of actual charts or maps drawn on paper or a board. They most often use a set of symbols or icons as a form of shorthand; for example, the simplest symbol is the arrow (→).

For example, a healthcare provider may have a relatively simple chart showing the progressive stages of a patient's journey through the system as he or she undergoes surgery. In super-simplified form, it might look like this:

Schedule → Preadmissions → Operating Room: Preparation, Sterilization Processing → Patient Registration → Inpatient Admission → Procedure → Recovery → Discharge.

Under each broad category you'd make lists of specific tasks to be completed, as well as links or connecting lines to employees or outside vendors who need to participate in each step. For example, under "Operating Room Preparation" you might see:

- Review pick lists for procedure equipment and supplies used.
- Procure any special equipment or supplies.
- Ensure staffing of the OR is commensurate with the procedure. Schedule any needed specialists.
- Ensure proper functioning of all *in situ* OR equipment.

Value stream mapping is especially useful in identifying and eliminating waste. Processes and items are mapped as either adding value or not adding value from the customer's perspective, with the goal of eliminating processes or items that don't add value. The value stream map needs to include all related processes, such as how customers order the product, both in frequency and method, which is then communicated back to the supplier. You should also include how you communicate requirements to your processes to ensure you produce exactly what the customer wants.

Because lean and Six Sigma share the same goal, which is to eliminate waste and create the most efficient system possible, value stream mapping has appeared in Six Sigma methodologies. But each approach takes a different stance toward identifying wasteful activities. While lean practitioners focus on activities that do not add value, Six Sigma practitioners focus more on process variations resulting in waste. Each has shown to be effective in different environments, leading to the creation of Lean Six Sigma, a combined approach.

Bear in mind that value stream mapping takes time and energy, and while it can be a powerful tool to identify waste, you don't want it to become a complicated end in itself. In other words, leaders need to be sure that VSM itself adds value and isn't simply an empty exercise designed to make leaders feel good about their management skills. They need to balance its potential value with the work necessary to conduct the VSM.

Scaling Agile

Being agile is pretty easy when you're a self-employed sole proprietor. You simply say, "Self, should we make this choice? Yes? Good—it's decided!"

It continues to be easy when your company or department has only a handful of team members. You can quickly get everyone together, discuss an idea, and make a decision.

But how can you stay agile when your organization scales up to one hundred or one thousand employees? Or one hundred thousand?

Now instead of driving a nimble speedboat, you're the captain of a massive ocean liner.

(By the way, the largest single employer in the world today is the United States Department of Defense, with 3.2 million employees stationed in every corner of the globe. But it's very different from the number two US employer, Walmart, which lists 2.3 million on its payroll: Unlike Walmart, the US military is a money loser that doesn't sell anything and isn't expected to earn revenues.)

Compared to small projects, which are ideal for agile development, larger and more complex projects require additional coordination. When applying agile to larger projects, handling interteam coordination becomes a particular challenge. Additional concerns with large-scale agile include interfacing with other organizational units such as human resources, marketing and sales, and product management. Scaling up may cause users and other stakeholders to have difficulty communicating with the growing development teams.

Despite these emerging problems related to scaled-up agile, industry is trending toward adopting agile methodologies in increasingly large contexts.

As Kim Dikert, Maria Paasivaara, and Casper Lassenius wrote in "Challenges and success factors for large-scale agile transformations: A systematic literature review," according to the 2016 "The State of Agile Survey" that Version One has been conducting annually since 2007, "62% of the almost 4,000 respondents had more than a hundred people in their software organization and 43% of all the respondents worked in development organizations where more than half of the teams were agile . . . This indicates that there seems to exist a large number of companies that have taken or are taking agile into use in large-scale settings."

Challenges of scaling agile include:

*   Increased size brings greater organizational inertia, slowing down organizational change.

*   Adopting agile often requires changing the entire organizational culture, which becomes more difficult as the organization gets larger.

*   Larger organizations have a greater need for formal documentation, which reduces agility.

*   Agile development teams may need to interact with other organizational units, such as human resources, that are often non-agile in nature.

*   Agile methods emphasize planning only for the near future, but the lack of long-range planning can be a concern when making business decisions that may affect thousands of employees.

Created by Dean Leffingwell and originally released in 2011, the Scaled Agile Framework (SAFe) is a comprehensive set of interactive graphical charts, discussions, and instructional courses intended to help businesses "address the significant challenges of developing and delivering enterprise-class software and systems in the shortest sustainable lead time . . . It's an online freely revealed knowledge base of proven, integrated patterns for implementing Lean-Agile development."

SAFe recognizes, and can used with, any one of four levels of organizational complexity:

1. **Team level.** SAFe is based on agile teams, which are responsible for delivering value in a series of fixed-length iterations, or sprints. An agile team typically has five to nine dedicated individual contributors who are responsible for building a quality increment of value for an iteration. These contributors include the scrum master, product owner, and various developers, testers, and specialists.

2. **Program level**, where teams are organized into a virtual program structure called the "Agile Release Train" (ART), which supports the enterprise's significant value streams. Comprised of cross-functional teams, each ART includes all the roles necessary to move ideas from concept through deployment.

3. **Value Stream level**, which supports the development of large and complex solutions requiring multiple, synchronized ARTs. This is optional in SAFe. Enterprises that can be built with a few hundred practitioners, or with systems that are largely independent, may not need these constructs.

4. **Portfolio level**, which organizes and funds a set of value streams. The value streams fulfill a set of solutions that help the enterprise achieve its strategic mission. In small to midsize companies, one SAFe portfolio may be all that's necessary, while in large enterprises, multiple SAFe portfolios—one for each line of business—may be required. "Portfolio epics" are large-enterprise initiatives, which, before implementation, require analysis of

cost, impact, and opportunity in a business case, followed by approval.

The Framework is scalable and modular, allowing each organization to adapt it to its own business model.

SAFe's proprietary interactive charts incorporate four levels of complexity, which the company calls:

1. Essential SAFe
2. Portfolio SAFe
3. Large Solution SAFe
4. Full SAFe

The charts include various icons, such as "Product Mgmt," "Backlog," and "Scrum Master," which the user can click on to reveal detailed explanations.

For example, the first level, "Essential SAFe," was developed in 2016 to present the most basic view of the Framework. Consisting of the team and program levels, plus a foundation, it identifies the ten elements necessary to achieve a positive outcome. They are:

1. Anchor the Transformation with SAFe Lean-Agile Principles.
2. Implement Real Agile Team and Trains.
3. Apply Cadence and Synchronization.
4. Create Alignment with Program Increment (PI) Planning.
5. Improve DevOps and Releasability.
6. Get Fast Feedback with System Demo.
7. Relentlessly Improve with Inspect and Adapt.
8. Dedicate Time for Innovation and Planning.

9. Enable Fast Feature Delivery with Architectural Runway.
10. Lead with Lean-Agile Leadership.

When the enterprise embeds these positive, action-oriented elements into each Agile Release Train in their portfolio, they are on the road to realizing the full benefits of SAFe. To get the practitioner started in the right direction, there's an overview followed by a self-assessment tool in which the user indicates the number of problems or symptoms currently present in the organization.

As Stephen Younge, product line director for Rally Software, wrote in 2013 on zdnet.com, "Not only can agile scale, but as the pace of change accelerates and consumerization impacts every corner of economy and government, agile may mean the difference between success and failure in the long run." He added that as an enterprise or project grows, the agile methodology may cause teams to lose sight of long-range goals, including strategic planning, database standards, architectural runway, dependencies, and managing demand. But agile has a fractal, scalable nature that welcomes growth. In agile, the same methodologies and tradeoffs remain in alignment with different levels of scale in the organization.

Is this happening in real life?

Yes.

Among many other corporations, Microsoft—the world's largest computer software company—has committed to scaling up agile approaches to the enterprise level. As the company revealed in a corporate post on March 23, 2017, entitled "Meeting the challenges of agile development at enterprise scale," the company has recognized and made a commitment to the agile methodology. The post reads, "Microsoft IT develops and maintains software services for different groups within Microsoft. Over the last several years as part of our move to modern engineering, all our teams have adopted agile methodology."

When scaling up agile for enterprise projects, Microsoft found the issues get bigger. With the ideal size for an agile team being five to nine members, if you increase the size of the teams, or you group teams under a single project umbrella, you may need to make substantive changes in how your organization operates. The company found out it takes longer to do everything, including changing culture throughout the organization. To solve the problem, they wrote, "We had to take a step back and figure out how to bridge the communication gap between leadership, stakeholders, and agile teams. We're working to remove roadblocks at the human level—to increase buy-in and get the vision across at all levels. Clear communication, mitigating dependencies, and resolving blocks is an evolving and recurring process. We treat this process in the backlog in the same way as the project." And, "Under scaled agile, we find that the teams where leadership best understands and participates in the process experience the greatest benefits."

What lessons has Microsoft learned? When scaling agile, the company learned that it needed to prioritize these three areas:

1. **Minimize dependencies.** A "dependency" is when several teams rely on one team for a deliverable. If that one team is late,

then the one delay hampers many teams. No one team should exclusively own any part of the overall project.

2. **Deliver value.** In the original agile model, a team delivered a minimal viable product to the customer. In the scaled-up agile model, the deliverable may be to another team—but there still needs to be a sharp focus on value, as if the other team were a paying customer.

3. **Mature and align as a team.** When agile teams operate with total autonomy and adopt their own cadence, tools, and processes, issues arise when you try to coordinate the work of those teams to deliver a large-scale product or suite of products. Teams need to be aligned so that they function as parts of a whole rather than as individual units each marching to the cadence of their own drummer.

Chapter 5:

Agile for the Long Term

As we've seen in this book, the agile methodology was not initially designed to shape or influence a company's long-term strategy. It began as a way to manage defined projects—specifically, the production of software application programs involving small teams writing millions of lines of code, which, after field testing a series of increasingly complex iterations, would eventually produce a finished product.

But the agile methodology has proven to be attractive to both large software companies like Microsoft and to companies that aren't in the software business. It is becoming a philosophy of general business management.

In making this migration, new concepts are emerging that add new dimensions to the agile methodology. One of them is the agile product road map.

As noted by Janna Bastow in her article "Agile Roadmapping: How To Think Big, Ship Fast And Always Keep Moving," the road map seeks to blend two distinct mandates: the need to make steady progress through incremental change, for which agile is well suited, and the need for breakthrough innovation that more closely resembles the old waterfall model of a massive push toward a singular outcome. "Agile product roadmapping helps you answer that question in safe, controlled iterations," she wrote. "From your vision, you set goals. From your goals, you define desired outcomes. Then you launch a series of experiments in sprints to meet those outcomes. If you meet them, you move onwards. If you don't? Take a coffee break, then pivot."

Agile road mapping lets you think both big and small, and supports the creation of elastic, vision-driven product teams. An agile road map helps you communicate both your long-range vision and the series of steps you anticipate will bring you to that vision. While the steps matter, they're flexible and even replaceable. Business conditions will change, new and unexpected technologies will emerge, and competitors will surge or suddenly fall back; and all of these shifts will influence what you create both in the short and long term.

An agile product road map is *goal oriented* and sometimes also referred to as *theme based*. These road maps focus on outcomes, goals, and objectives, such as increasing engagement, acquiring customers, and removing technical debt. Features are still important, but they are derived from, and serve, the goals.

A product vision board can help you develop a viable product strategy by capturing the problem to be solved, the target group, the vision, or the benefit to be provided, as well as the business goals and the key features of the product. The agile product road map should be kept simple and easy to understand. Incorporate only what's most important by focusing on the goals and leaving out extraneous details.

Specific features on your road map should be rough-sketched and relate directly to the goals.

Be selective. As Steve Jobs said, "Innovation is not about saying 'yes' to everything. It's about saying 'no' to all but the most crucial features."

The Center of Excellence

To manage and promote the agile approach within a large organization, it may be useful to create a center of excellence (CoE, also known as a competency center or a capability center).

A center of excellence is a team, a shared facility, or another community resource that within a focus area provides leadership, best practices, research, support, and/or training. The focus area might be a business concept such as agile, but it could also serve a technology, a skill, or a broad area of study. It's anything that's important enough to the business to devote the necessary resources.

A business CoE may provide training, guidance, support, research, and oversight for employees or team members. A CoE may be ongoing or temporary, and group members may work in another capacity or be full time in the CoE.

Some common examples of centers of excellence are:

Six Sigma – This is perhaps the most mature of the CoEs embraced by many organizations. Invented by Motorola and popularized by GE, in many companies the Six Sigma CoE has grown into a strategic asset that drives competitiveness and differentiation. It generally includes a well-understood methodology (DMAIC); formal certified roles, including Champions, Sponsors, and Black Belts; a standard set of tools such as statistical control; and an active community.

Agile – The agile CoE is a group that fosters and spreads the adoption of the agile movement within a company by identifying, collecting, and communicating the best practices employed by teams within the company so that teams have solutions available to help with their own experiments.

Business Analysis – Some organizations have used a CoE to address business requirements, especially around software development. A certification for Business Analysts from the IIBA has further validated this idea.

Project Management Office (PMO) – The most successful PMOs grow beyond that single focus and take on a full CoE role around project management.

Process – Since all businesses are made up of processes, this could be the most strategic of all CoEs. It allows for all the traditional focus of lean and Six Sigma as well as for creating new strategies and business capabilities.

There are many more.

Agile Goes Mainstream

What began in 2001 as a specific approach to the development of new software programs has spread to a wide variety of other industries, and in the years ahead it's expected to find increasing mainstream acceptance.

As Darrell K. Rigby, Jeff Sutherland, and Hirotaka Takeuchi wrote in "Embracing Agile" for the *Harvard Business Review*, the agile approach is being seen in unexpected places, including National Public Radio, which employs agile methods to create new programming; C.H. Robinson, a global third-party logistics provider, where they're being applied in human resources; and Mission Bell Winery, which uses them for a range of functions including wine production, warehousing, and running its senior leadership group.

Innovation is at the heart of agile, and therefore the method is less useful in routine, repetitive processes and operations. But guess what? Because of the increasing rate of change in business and product life cycles, most companies need to continually innovate, and not just necessarily in their products—although product life cycles are getting shorter and new products are needed more quickly than ever—but in other functional areas as well.

For any company that needs to keep innovating just to stay competitive, the agile approach can have great value.

To capitalize on agile, leaders need to take these steps:

1. **Understand what agile can do and can't do.** It's like any other tool—to get the most out of it, you need to learn how to use it.
2. **Start narrow and expand.** Agile began as a system for project management. Set up a small test project and use it to see what agile can do for your organization.
3. **Give it time to settle in.** The longer people have to learn how to leverage an agile approach, the better they'll get at it. It's like learning any other new skill—it doesn't happen overnight!

4. **Take it to the C-suite!** Agile has applications for senior leaders, and if they're doing it, then they'll have a better understanding of how the process works and the experiences of their project teams.

As the twenty-first century unfolds, leaders will need to be well prepared to meet the challenges of increased competition, more consumer leverage, and a high rate of disruption. But with the right training and insights, and the knowledgeable application of agile methods, sustained market domination can be a reality.

Thank You

Thank you for reading this book! For further information about this book please email doctoraleditor@gmail.com

About the Author

Gail Ferreira is an enterprise lean agile leader and enterprise agile coach based in San Francisco. Gail likes to employ creative and novel lean agile methods to engage individuals and organizations through agile transformations. She is particularly passionate about creating agile learning organizations that embrace continuous learning and change management using a blend of lean and agile methodologies.

Gail regularly speaks at international agile conferences and professional groups related to agile, innovation, lean startup, strategy, and technology management. She has published peer-reviewed journals and articles in award-winning publications such as *Agile Connection*, *Proquest Digital Dissertations*, *Refractive Thinker*, *IEEE*, and *Techwell*. Gail also likes to lead and direct events including local meetups, professional development days for the Project Management Institute, and academic awards.

Gail is an adjunct professor and advisor at UC Berkeley Extension Agile Specialist program and Capella University PhD in Technology and Project Management, where she mentors aspiring doctoral candidates with their dissertation publications for the School Of Information Technology Management.

LinkedIn Profile: https://www.linkedin.com/in/drgail.ferreira

Education, PhD – Organizational Leadership, M.S. Computer Science, B.S. Computer Science

Certifications: SAFe-SPC, Lean Six Sigma Black Belt, CSP, CSM, CSPO, PMP

Appointments: Enterprise Agile Track Chair – Agile 2018, VP of Professional Development – Project Management Institute – 2016

Made in the USA
Middletown, DE
18 October 2020

22294561R00042